MASON

AND THE PANDEMIC

MASON
AND THE PANDEMIC

WRITTEN BY PAMELLA FINE

EDITED AND ILLUSTRATED BY CADENCE PARAMORE

gatekeeper press™
Columbus, Ohio

Mason and The Pandemic

Published by Gatekeeper Press
2167 Stringtown Rd, Suite 109
Columbus, OH 43123-2989
www.GatekeeperPress.com

Library of Congress Control Number: 2020942031

ISBN (hardcover): 9781662902949
ISBN (paperback): 9781662902956
eISBN: 9781662902963

My name is Mason and I'm 6½ years old. I live with my older brother, Zach, who is 11½, and our parents whose ages I better keep quiet about.

We also have a bulldog named Kona!
She's only a few months old!

I know I also haven't lived
very much of my life yet,

but I have all these different thoughts about
things that have been happening recently.

For instance, my world has changed
because of what I like to call,

"THE CORONA."

Before this Pandemic, I could ride the school bus to Kindergarten- my favorite part of the day!

I could be with my friends, learning and playing,

or sometimes talking too much and not putting
my listening ears on in class.

I could eat a peanut butter sandwich every day,

or sometimes I could buy pizza for lunch!

I LOVE pizza!

I used to go to Karate twice a week.
I'm pretty good at it!

I was also learning how to play LaCrosse just like Zach does! He's really good at that!

I could have real play dates with my friends—not just on Zoom.

And if Mom said a movie was appropriate, we could go to the movie theater and get candy and sit in big chairs that move with buttons I could press!

My family also loves to go out to eat, even though I've been told I'm a very picky eater.

We used to go to Grandma's for dinner once a week,
she always makes me things I like.

And it is *always* a dessert night at her house!
Now we can't go anywhere . . .

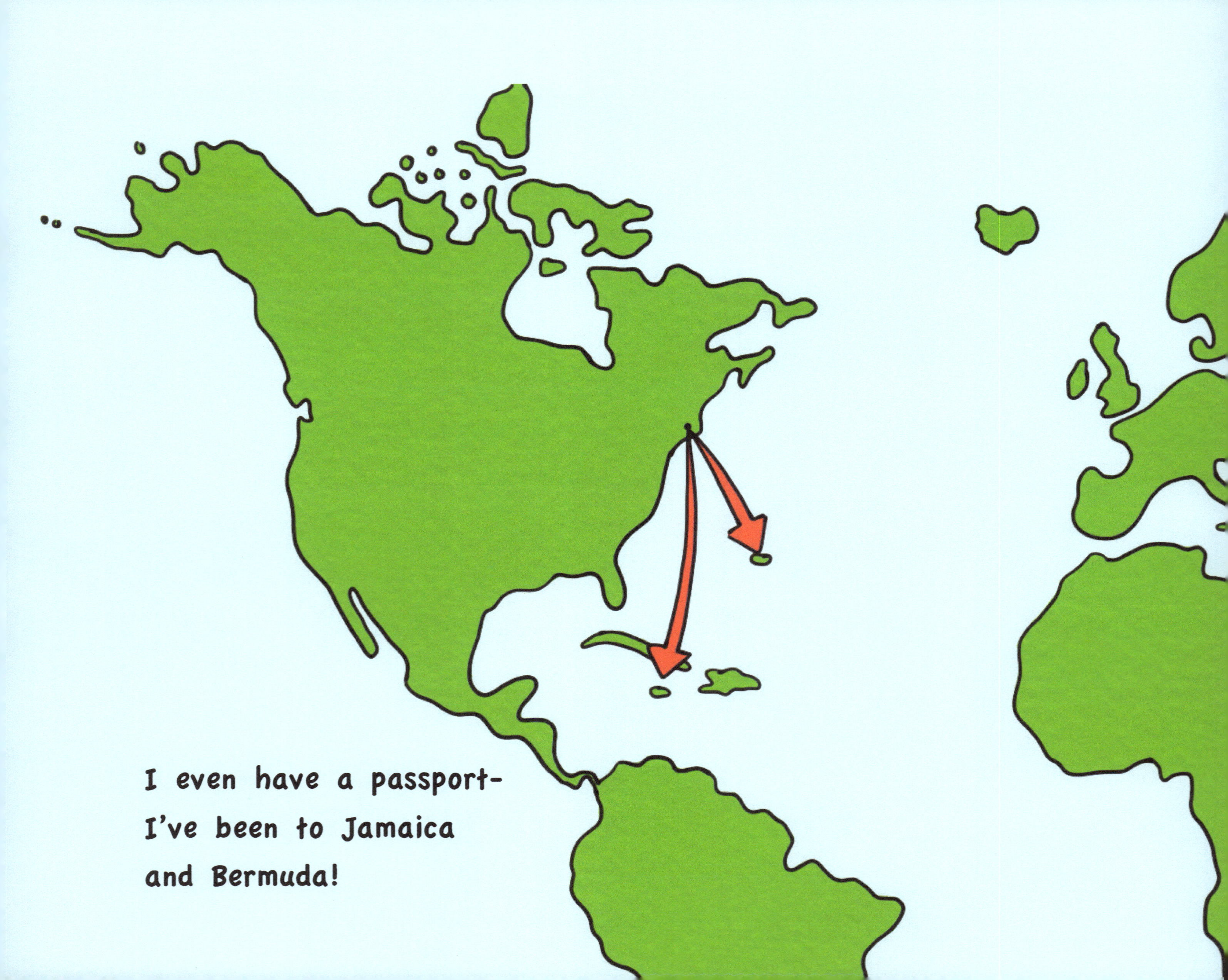

I even have a passport-
I've been to Jamaica
and Bermuda!

I love flying on airplanes, especially ones with your own TV and great snacks!

I guess what I'm trying to tell you is that my life was pretty great before "The Corona."

Nobody seems to know when my world will
go back to the way it was.

I worry that someone I know might get sick.
Mom has me wash my hands so many times a
day that I worry I'll rub my skin right off.

People walk by my house wearing masks and gloves.
That's fun on Halloween, but it's scary now.

Zach is very smart; he doesn't seem to see the world the way I do. He doesn't seem scared.

He told me to make a list of all the things I'm scared of, and he would write them down for me. He said that when you say your fears out loud and then talk about them, they really don't seem so scary. So here goes . . .

Wow- I didn't realize I had such a long list of fears.

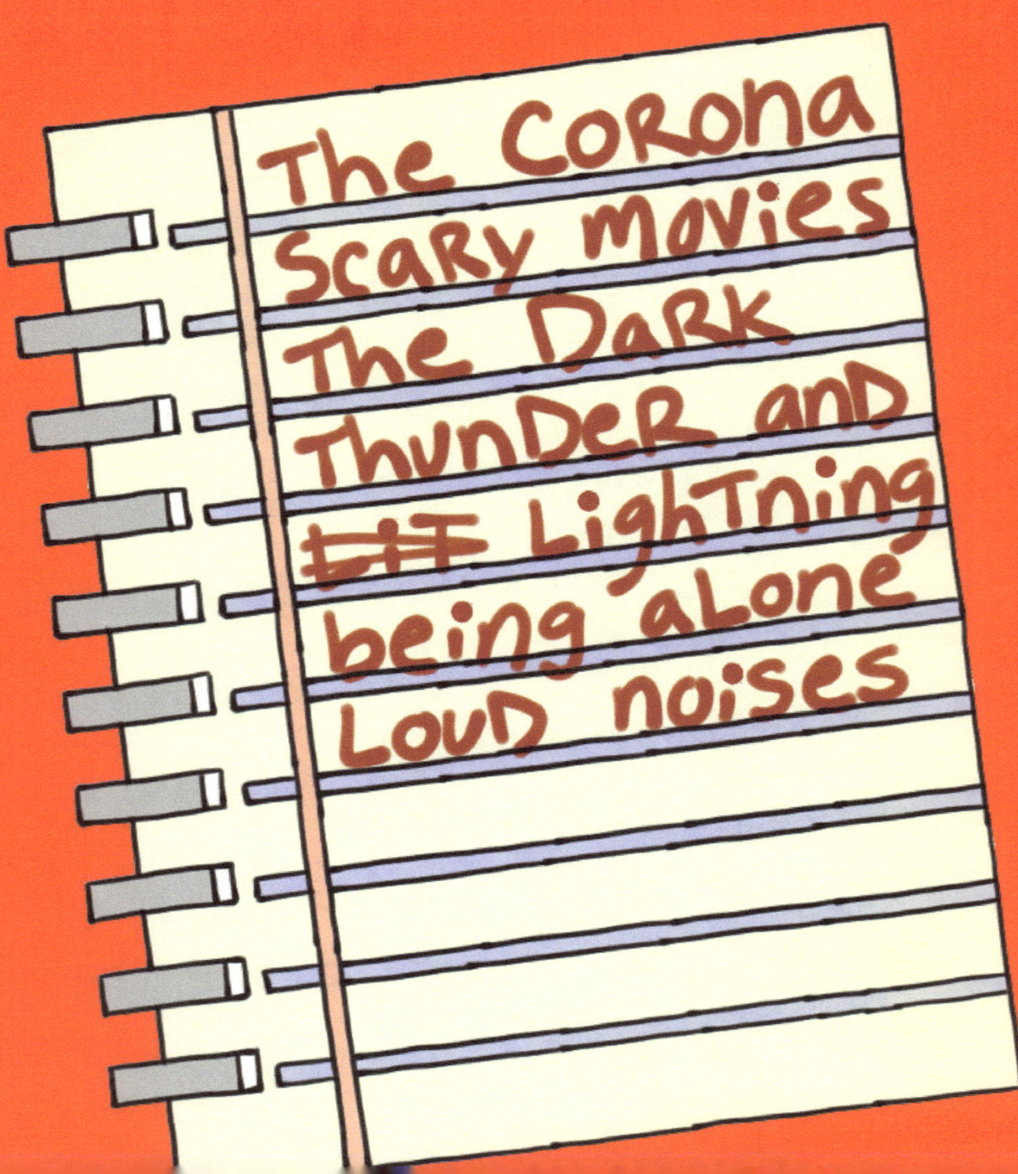

Something amazing happened after I made this list. Zach told me that fears are really just thoughts that seem bigger than they actually are. When you talk about them with your family, you are calming down your "inner brain," as Zach calls it.

I'm going to try to remember this when we get back to what big people keep saying will be "the new normal."

I guess my world really is still pretty great!